ARGENTINA

in pictures

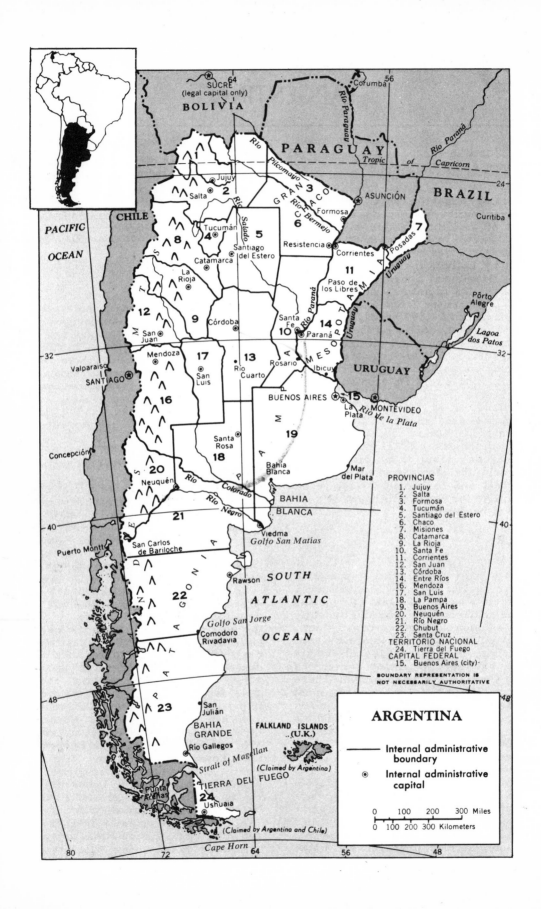

ARGENTINA

PROVINCIAS
1. Jujuy
2. Salta
3. Formosa
4. Tucumán
5. Santiago del Estero
6. Chaco
7. Misiones
8. Catamarca
9. La Rioja
10. Santa Fe
11. Corrientes
12. San Juan
13. Córdoba
14. Entre Ríos
15. Mendoza
16. San Luis
17. La Pampa
18. Buenos Aires
19. Neuquén
20. Río Negro
21. Chubut
22. Santa Cruz
23. Santa Cruz

TERRITORIO NACIONAL
24. Tierra del Fuego

CAPITAL FEDERAL
15. Buenos Aires (city)

BOUNDARY REPRESENTATION IS
NOT NECESSARILY AUTHORITATIVE

———— Internal administrative
boundary

⊙ Internal administrative
capital

0   100   200   300 Miles

0   100 200 300 Kilometers

ARGENTINA

in pictures

Prepared by E. W. EGAN

VISUAL
GEOGRAPHY
SERIES

STERLING PUBLISHING CO., INC.
NEW YORK

The Oak Tree Press
LONDON AND SYDNEY

VISUAL GEOGRAPHY SERIES

Alaska
Argentina
Australia
Austria
Belgium and Luxembourg
Berlin—East and West
Brazil
Canada
Ceylon
Chile
Denmark
England
Finland
France
French Canada
Ghana
Greece

Guatemala
Hawaii
Holland
Hong Kong
India
Ireland
Israel
Italy
Jamaica
Japan
Malaysia and Singapore
Mexico
Morocco
New Zealand
Norway
Peru
The Philippines

Portugal
Puerto Rico
Russia
Scotland
Spain
Sweden
Switzerland
Tahiti and the
    French Islands of
    the Pacific
Thailand
Turkey
Venezuela
Wales
West Germany
Yugoslavia

PICTURE CREDITS

The publishers wish to thank the following for the use of the photographs in this book: Argentine Consulate, New York; Argentine Embassy, London; Argentine Embassy, Washington; Braniff Airways; Canadian Pacific; Coca-Cola International; Foto Archivo, Buenos Aires; Moore-McCormack Lines; Museum of the American Indian, Heye Foundation, New York; Panagra; Pan American Airways; Pan American Union; United Nations; Varig Airlines.

The Obelisk in the Plaza de Republica rises above the business district of Buenos Aires.

CONTENTS

In the dry hills of Mendoza Province, the llama is a familiar domestic animal, and one of the few to have been tamed by the aboriginal Indians of America.

The pampa, once treeless and unfenced, now has enclosures such as this, rimmed with willows as a windbreak, to contain the spirited horses of the gauchos.

I. THE LAND

ARGENTINA lies in the southern part of South America, stretching from the tropical wilderness of the Gran Chaco in the north to within 100 miles of Cape Horn, the chilly tip of the continent, close to Antarctic waters. With an area of almost 1,100,000 square miles, it is exceeded in size by only one other Latin American country—Brazil. It is almost one-third as large as the United States of America and more than ten times as large as the United Kingdom.

TOPOGRAPHY

Within the vaguely carrot-shaped boundaries of the Argentine Republic there is a remarkable range of terrain and natural conditions. People often think of the Republic in terms of the *pampas*, or grasslands, where some of the finest beef in the world is grown, but the pampas are only one part of the landscape.

Running down the entire western boundary of the country is the breathtaking chain of the

The peak of Tronador, capped with snow and framed in native conifers, rises above the clear waters of Lake Nahuel-huapi in the central Andes.

A road cuts a thin white ribbon against the hillside in the high, dry, many-ridged plateau of Uspallata where highland meets the Mendoza Plain.

On the low-lying coastline between the pampa and the sea, the fashionable resort city of Mar del Plata boasts handsome modern buildings and broad sandy beaches.

Andes Mountains, many of their caps covered with perpetual snow, and many of their valleys choked with glacial ice. Here, near the frontier with Chile, is Mount Aconcagua (23,080 feet), an extinct volcano and the highest mountain in the New World. In the whole world, only the Himalayas of India and Tibet are higher than the Andes.

The Gran Chaco, occupying most of the northern part of the country, east of the Andes, is a broad lowland, whose forests thin out to the south, where they merge into the grasslands of the central region. Near the southern coast of Buenos Aires Province, the level *pampa* is broken by low mountain ridges (*c.* 3,000 feet) running east to west. Farther south lies the great tableland of Patagonia, and finally, across the Strait of Magellan, the large island of Tierra del Fuego, whose eastern half is Argentine territory. The western half is owned by Chile,

as are numerous lesser islands, on one of which is situated Cape Horn.

The lowest point on the continent of South America is Salinas Grandes, on the Valdès Peninsula—131 feet below sea level. This peninsula on the northern coast of Patagonia is itself virtually an island—a round chunk of land connected to the mainland by the thinnest of land bridges.

BOUNDARIES

Besides Chile, the countries bordering upon Argentina are Bolivia and Paraguay on the north, and Brazil and Uruguay on the northeast. The greater part of the frontiers with all these countries consists of rivers, except for the Bolivian boundary, which cuts across the Andes chain.

From north to south the greatest distance is about 2,300 miles. The Atlantic Ocean forms

9

Driftwood piles up at Ventisquero Moreno in Santa Cruz Province.

la Plata south, the coast is scalloped by a succession of wide-mouthed bays—Bahia Blanca, Golfo San Matías, Golfo San Jorge, and Bahia Grande.

In addition to its home territory, Argentina claims a large sweep of the coast of Antarctica opposite Cape Horn, and various islands in between, but these claims are not recognized by the United States and the Soviet Union (neither of which recognizes the claim of any country to Antarctic territory). Furthermore, the Argentine claims are in conflict with those of Chile and Great Britain.

BUENOS AIRES

Capital and largest city of the Argentine Republic is Buenos Aires, one of the greatest commercial hubs of the world. It is situated on the Río de la Plata, where the pampa meets the sea. A city of broad boulevards and spacious squares, its architecture recalls that of Paris, especially those parts of Paris that were built in the late 19th and early 20th centuries. Those were the years in which Buenos Aires rose from a minor capital to a metropolis. European immigrant stock of non-Spanish origin helped make the city great, and they and the Spanish colonists who had broken the tie with Spain looked to France for cultural inspiration.

the greater part of the eastern limit of Argentina —a total of 1,600 miles of coastline, most of which is of low altitude. Several great bays indent the seacoast, the most important being the Río de la Plata (Silver River), which lies between Argentina and Uruguay. The Río de la Plata, in spite of its name, is an estuary, into which empties one of the great river systems of South America—the Paraná. From the Río de

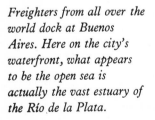

Freighters from all over the world dock at Buenos Aires. Here on the city's waterfront, what appears to be the open sea is actually the vast estuary of the Río de la Plata.

A panoramic view of central Buenos Aires shows some tall buildings, but fewer than in other New World cities of comparable size. The Porteños, as the people of Buenos Aires are called, like the Parisians, have been reluctant to alter their skyline.

It is a city of great vitality—the main seaport and financial capital of Argentina, and the principal clearing house for the fortunes in beef, hides, mutton, wool, wheat, maize, and flax produced in the interior. It is also the focal point of Argentine industry, education, culture, and science.

The more than 3,000,000 citizens of the city make good use of its fine parks, public gardens and tree-lined streets, where they enjoy the advantages of a delightful climate. The city, in fact, owes its name ("good air" in Spanish) to its climate.

The heart of the business district of Buenos Aires has narrow streets going off in many directions rather like London's City or New York's Wall Street district.

Broad squares with fountains and trees are common in Buenos Aires, as here in the Plaza del Congreso, before the Federal Capitol.

In the Plaza de Mayo in Buenos Aires, palm trees, pigeons, strollers and benches seating lookers-on combine to create an effect of tranquillity in the heart of one of the world's greatest cities.

Just off the Calle Florida in Buenos Aires, a side street bristling with small shops and overhung with neon signs is given over entirely to pedestrians.

Modern apartment houses rise above the older buildings of historic Mendoza. Although in the dry zone, the city is surrounded by an oasis fed by the Mendoza River, and is the hub of a thriving trade in wine, fruit and grain.

OTHER CITIES

Rosario (700,000) is the nation's second largest city. Situated on the Paraná River, it ships grain, hides, meat, and flaxseed from its busy wharves, while its factories mill flour, refine sugar, and process meat. Córdoba (600,000), splendidly situated between the pampa and the foothills of the Andes, is the commercial capital of the northwest, a great market for grain, cattle, and fruit, and a growing industrial city. Santa Fé (275,000) is a major river port on the Paraná north of Rosario; and Mar del Plata (330,000), on the coast south of the La Plata estuary, is a well-known resort, seaport, and food-processing city. Mendoza (250,000), the market-place for much of Argentina's large output of wine, lies deep in

the arid western uplands, but is surrounded by large areas of irrigated farmland. Tucumán (261,000), several hundred miles to the north of Mendoza, also lies in an "oasis" of irrigated farms—but the chief crop is sugar cane rather than grapes.

Other places of interest include Bahia Blanca (115,000), the finest natural port in Argentina. Long held back from full development by its remoteness from the concentration of people and industry to the north, the city has become a principal outlet for the oil of Patagonia. Ushuaia, while not a city, is the capital of the Territory of Tierra del Fuego. With about 1,200 people it bases its claim to being the southernmost town in the world on the fact that the few communities farther south are mere hamlets.

Paraná (103,000) is an important city on the

These falls in the Iguazú (Portuguese: Iguassú) River, a tributary of the Paraná, on the boundary of Brazil and Argentina, are shared by both countries. The Argentine side is a National Park. One of the marvels of South America, the Iguazú Falls are higher and wider than Niagara (only a part is seen here) and are set amid forests of the utmost sub-tropical beauty, alive with birds, butterflies and flowering plants.

river of the same name, and capital of the Province of Entre Ríos. It also lays claim to the title of chief city of Mesopotamia. Entre Ríos and Mesopotamia both mean "between rivers." Argentines have taken the name of the Middle East land between the Tigris and Euphrates, and applied it to that part of their own territory between the Paraná and Uruguay Rivers, which also includes the Province of Corrientes.

La Plata (410,000), just south of Buenos Aires, is a relatively new city, laid out in the 1880's to become the capital of Buenos Aires Province and thus remove some of the administrative burdens from the city of Buenos Aires. During his dictatorship, Juan Perón renamed the city Eva Perón, in homage to his wife, but after the downfall of Perón in 1955, the old name was restored.

The renaming of La Plata was not an innovation: many Argentine towns bear the names of people who figured in the country's history. In the United States and Australia, towns named in this way would usually consist only of the person's family name, either alone or with an ending such as -ville, -town, or -burg. But in Argentina the place name often includes the

A yacht docks at Modesta Victoria on the shores of Lake Nahuel-huapi near the boundary between the Provinces of Nequén and Río Negro.

14

The wind ripples the waters of Lake Gutierrez in the central Andean Province of Nequén. Argentine lakes of size are found mainly in the Andes and their foothills. The plains or pampas, on the other hand, are dotted with tiny lakes too small to be shown on the average map.

Christian name or the title of the person commemorated. Comodoro (Commodore) Rivadavia, Antonio de Biedma, Coronel (Colonel) Pringels, and General Madariaga all appear on the map of Argentina!

RIVERS AND LAKES

The Paraná system, which drains northern and much of central Argentina, has three main divisions: the Paraná proper, the Paraguay, and the Uruguay, all of which rise in Brazil. In the Gran Chaco region, where the Paraguay and its tributary, the Pilcomayo, divide the Republic of Paraguay from Argentina, there are vast swamps.

Of the rivers to the south of this great system, the most important are the Negro and the Colorado, which drain the eastern slopes of the Andes and flow eastward across northern

Patagonia to the Atlantic. It is a curious fact of South American geography that both these rivers rise within a relatively short distance of the Pacific Ocean but because of the great mountain wall, must seek outlets hundreds of miles to the east, crossing arid regions where their volume of water is often greatly reduced before being discharged into the Atlantic.

Another peculiarity of the drainage of southern Argentina is a series of lakes, some of which drain into the Pacific, through the steep valleys of Chile, but which, after heavy rains, may send excess water towards the Atlantic. This happens because the lakes are located almost upon the continental divide. The most beautiful of Argentine lakes is Nahuel-huapi, about 200 square miles in area, and 2,000 feet above sea level, in the southern Andes, often compared to the Swiss lakes.

15

Before the San Martín Memorial in Buenos Aires, people bask in the warm sun, but they are warmly dressed for the most part, for there is a nip in the air. The mild climate of northern Argentina makes out-of-door's activity possible the year round.

CLIMATE

Most of Argentina is in the south temperate zone, but there are considerable variations in temperature. The Andean regions vary from cool in the north to quite cold in the south. The northern lowlands are tropical. The central lowlands and pampas are moderate, similar to southern Europe, while the Patagonian steppe is wild and windy. Tierra del Fuego is cold and foggy, one of the least inviting parts of the country, but by no means uninhabitable, since ocean currents temper the climate, especially on the coast.

In general, rainfall diminishes towards the Andean chain. The winds from the Atlantic

have discharged most of their water clouds by the time they reach the great mountain divide, while those from the Pacific pour rain upon the western or Chilean side of the mountains. The rest of the rain falls on the Argentine Andes and little is left over for the Argentine plains. Consequently, most of western Argentina tends to be arid, with rivers that run dry and disappear into salt flats, and parched foothills of little value for farming or stock-raising. The westward decrease in rainfall is reflected in the division of the central plain into the "wet" and "dry" (eastern and western) pampas.

Since Argentina lies wholly in the southern hemisphere, January is the warmest month and July the coldest. The winter months (June, July

In Salta Province there are many stretches of very arid country, where water supply is a problem. This scene of a bridge spanning the dry bed of a stream is typical of the Andes and adjacent regions of northern Argentina.

and August) are also the driest. The climate of the heavily populated east central region is healthy and bracing throughout the year, averaging in the low 70's in summer and the high 40's in winter.

VEGETATION

In the lush forests of the northeast, bordering on Paraguay and Brazil, many species of tropical and subtropical plants grow together. Along with the more usual hardwood trees is found a species of Araucaria, a conifer related to the familiar "monkey puzzle" tree or Chile pine, introduced into gardens in the milder parts of the British Isles and the United States.

The northern lowlands support a varied flora. In the east a typical plant, and an important one in everyday Argentine life, is the yerba mate or Paraguay tea, a kind of holly whose leaves are infused like tea leaves. Westward the Chaco region open savannas alternate with woodland, some of it scrubby.

Horses cluster in a corral against a background of mountains and poplar windbreaks in the Province of Río Negro, a scene reminiscent of the North American West.

An important tree of these parts is the red quebracho, whose bark and heartwood furnish tannin, an essential substance in treating leather, and whose hard wood has many uses, even being made into paving blocks.

Except where they have been introduced by farmers and ranchers, trees are not found in the pampa. This vast area was originally one great expanse of tall grass, thinning to the west, where it merges into the thorny brush of the arid belt.

Patagonia's plateaus are given over to shrubby plants, seldom more than a few feet tall, of types able to withstand both drought and wind. It is curious that the aboriginal Indians of this land of low-growing plants and few large animals were one of the tallest races in the New World. These people, the Tehuelches, were long known as the Patagonian Giants, owing to the greatly exaggerated reports of their stature by early European explorers.

The Andes of Argentina are densely forested throughout their entire length, except for some parts in the far north where cactus scrub prevails. Elsewhere in the northern Andes, where rain is plentiful, are found large stands of trees, notably the yew-like Podocarpus. Southward the high-altitude forest consists of both conifers and trees that shed their leaves—the Chilean *arbor vitae* and the Fitzroy cypress being the most common evergreens, and the false beech a typical deciduous tree of the region.

WILDLIFE

Argentina shares with the rest of South America a relative scarcity of large land animals. The two largest—the vegetarian tapir and the meat-eating jaguar—are most typical of the tropical parts of the continent, but are found in northern Argentina also. Other warm-climate animals living in the wilder reaches of the Paraná and Paraguay River basin are the giant anteater and the capybara, the world's largest rodent (as large as a pig). In nearly all parts of the country the puma or mountain lion is to be found. This tawny predator is only about half the size of the jaguar, which is the largest American member of the cat family, exceeding in size the leopard of the Old World.

In the Andes and the dry plateaus and plains adjoining them the most distinctive animal is

In the arid Andes of northern Argentina a herd of llamas, some wearing packs, pad over the stony soil. A domestic animal of the camel family, the llama was the chief form of livestock kept by the ancient Incas and other Indians of the Andes. It still serves as a beast of burden and a source of wool, milk and meat.

the guanaco, a small humpless New World kin of the camel, and wild relative of the domestic llama and alpaca. Some zoologists regard the latter two creatures as tamed descendants of the guanaco.

Patagonia and the pampas are home to a very large number of rodent species. The Patagonian cavy, relative of the guinea pig, belies that relationship with its long legs and rather harelike appearance. The viscacha is a busy burrower of the pampa, building enormous underground networks like those of the North American prairie dog. Many a horseman has cursed the viscacha after his horse has broken a leg plunging it into a burrow.

The plains are the home of the swift-footed rhea, a large flightless bird resembling the ostrich. Among the many other birds of Argentina are the crested screamer, a running bird of the plains, and the succulent tinamou, an esteemed game bird resembling a grouse, but actually a member of the ostrich group.

Downy clouds drift across the sky as a horse drinks his fill from one of the myriad ponds of the well-watered eastern pampa.

On the pampa not far from Buenos Aires, gauchos drive cows and their calves towards the paddock for weighing.

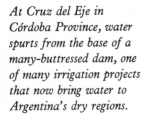

At Cruz del Eje in Córdoba Province, water spurts from the base of a many-buttressed dam, one of many irrigation projects that now bring water to Argentina's dry regions.

Cattle are the lifeblood of Argentina—more than 40,000,000 of them graze on the pampa. Ceaseless research in breeding and animal hygiene is applied towards keeping the quality of the stock high. Here at the Balcarce Agricultural Experiment Station, Black Angus cattle huddle in a paddock.

NATURAL RESOURCES

Although Argentina and its great La Plata estuary both bear names that mean "silver," the country is not at present a major source of that metal. Indeed, mining is not an important industry at all, unless petroleum exploitation is included in that category. Oil-bearing strata have been drilled profitably since the beginning of the 20th century, mainly in the vicinity of Comodoro Rivadavia in Patagonia, but also in the far north in the Province of Salta, and in the middle Andean Province of Nequén.

Salt is mined on a large scale for domestic consumption. Small quantities of other minerals are obtained in different parts of the country—sulphur, borates, asbestos, gold, copper, marble, tin, zinc, and lead, but production of none of these is sufficient to supply local needs, much less support an export trade. There is a fair amount of low-grade coal, but this also is far from meeting the nation's requirements.

Forests account for more than 30 per cent of the area of the country, but do not produce any important export item except quebracho extract.

The greatest resources of Argentina are its enormous grazing lands, home of one of the largest and finest cattle industries in the world; and its vast regions of rich topsoil, one of the great grain-producing regions of the globe.

In the Battle of Maipú on April 5, 1818, San Martín smashed the power of Spain in the south of South America forever and the way was open for his grand scheme to materialize—the conquest of Peru, the citadel of Spanish power in the New World.

2. HISTORY

THE FIRST RECORDED VISIT by Europeans to Argentina took place in 1516, when Juan Díaz de Solís entered the Río de la Plata and claimed its shores for Spain. It is thought, however, that Amerigo Vespucci may have sailed into the great estuary, whose existence he noted during his voyage of exploration for Portugal in 1502.

In 1520, the Portuguese explorer, Ferdinand Magellan, sailing for Spain, stopped at the Río de la Plata on his historic voyage round the world. Then in 1526, Sebastian Cabot, an Italian in the service of Spain at the time, sailed into the estuary and up the Paraná River, where he established the first temporary European settlement on the soil of Argentina, not far from the site of the present city of Rosario. Cabot found the native Indians wearing silver ornaments and sent some of the bangles to Spain. This, perhaps, explains the name Río de

la Plata (silver river), which thereafter appeared on maps, replacing the earlier Río de Solís.

Spanish colonization began in earnest after Francisco Pizarro conquered the Inca Empire of Peru in 1532. Of the many expeditions to South America that followed that historic conquest, one, in 1536, resulted in a temporary settlement on the site of Buenos Aires. Constant attack by the Indians, famine, and disease led to the abandonment of the colony in 1541.

EARLY COLONIAL PERIOD

A permanent colony, however, had been established at Asunción in what is now Paraguay, and the Argentine lands, on paper at least, were governed from there. Tucumán was founded in 1565, Córdoba in 1573, and then in 1580 a lasting settlement was made at Buenos Aires by

Fanciful pottery jars are among articles of artistic merit made by the Indians.

Juan de Garay of the Asunción colony. By this time Spain had organized all of its South American lands into one single viceroyalty, governed from Peru, and Argentina fell under the jurisdiction of a sub-division of the vast realm with headquarters in what is now Bolivia. Spanish rule was directed towards one goal— the enrichment of Spain. The Creoles, or colonists, many of whom were American-born at this point, usually had little voice in the government.

However, in 1617, Hernando Arias de Saavedra, a son-in-law of Garay and a native of Asunción, managed to secure local government for Buenos Aires, including much of what is now Argentina.

LATER COLONIAL PERIOD

The Spaniards imposed severe restrictions on trade and the movement of goods in South America. Shipping was banned from the Río de la Plata, and such Buenos Aires merchandise as hides and tallow (the cattle industry was already thriving) was obliged to travel overland through the Andes to Panama, 2,000 miles away. Similarly, much-needed imports could not be brought by ship directly to Buenos Aires, but had to go to Panama, there to be forwarded by the same tedious and dangerous route. The result of this imposition was that Buenos Aires became a smugglers' haven and headquarters for a profitable trade in illicit goods.

Arrowheads of bone, such as these from the Paraná delta, are typical of the weapons used by Argentina's Indian aborigines.

23

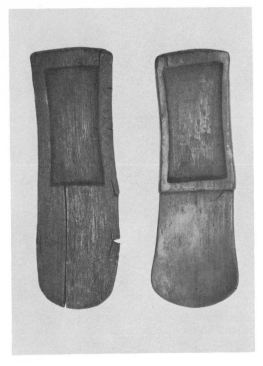

Wooden snuff trays were made by Argentine Indians, as were bells, dishes and implements designed to fit over the knuckles.

The early settlers of Argentina were in large part descended from the Spanish colonists in Paraguay, a sturdy breed in whose veins flowed the blood of the Guàrani Indians who had freely intermarried with the white settlers of Asunción. From them came the first *gauchos*, the hardy cattlemen of the pampa, who often showed a dash of Indian blood. These cowboys and the

Indian skeletons from the Paraná delta symbolize the fate of Argentina's primitive Indian population—virtual annihilation.

José de San Martín entered the service of the King of Spain at the age of 12, and had had 22 years of military experience when, still a young man, he took up the cause of South American independence in 1812. He ultimately liberated Argentina, Chile, and Peru.

smuggler merchants of Buenos Aires had less and less sympathy with Spanish rule.

The Spaniards finally recognized the need for local government in the colonies on the Río de la Plata, and in 1776 created the Viceroyalty of La Plata, with Buenos Aires as its capital. They also made the city a free port, thus putting an end to the smugglers' trade. These measures brought about a rapid increase in commerce and population.

INDEPENDENCE

Although Buenos Aires prospered under relaxed Spanish rule, its people were still not satisfied to remain governed by an overseas power. The successful revolt of England's colonies in North America and the republican spirit of the French Revolution influenced many of the Argentine colonists to question the right of Madrid to control their affairs.

In the meantime, Napoleon had conquered half of Europe, and Spain, entering into alliance with him, declared war on England in 1804. In 1806, following the disastrous defeat of the combined French and Spanish fleets off Trafalgar, the English sent an expeditionary force to Buenos Aires and occupied the city. The colonists, under Santiago de Liniers and Martín Alzaga, rose up in arms and expelled the English. Then, in 1808, Napoleon occupied Spain and put his brother on the throne.

On May 25, 1810, the Spanish Viceroy in Buenos Aires was ousted. In 1960, the 150th anniversary of that event was commemorated by the Patricians Regiment, Argentina's most exclusive military body.

The meeting between San Martín and Manuel Belgrano at Yatasta in 1814 was depicted by the 19th-century artist, Agosto Ballerini. San Martín replaced Belgrano as leader of the revolutionary forces in Upper Peru, as Bolivia was then called. Belgrano, an Argentine, later devoted his energies to attacking Uruguay.

Buenos Aires was left to its own devices. By 1810, the colonists had acquired a taste for self-rule, and organized their own government under a junta of local citizens. The new government professed to rule in the name of the Spanish throne, but paid no heed to Madrid even after the downfall of Napoleon.

In 1816, independence from Spain was formally declared. The Viceroyalty of La Plata had included Paraguay and Uruguay, but these countries went their own way, Paraguay becoming independent in 1811, and Uruguay embarking in 1814 on a long struggle for freedom. The Spaniards remained entrenched in Chile, Bolivia, and Peru.

JOSE DE SAN MARTIN

At this point one of South America's great liberators emerged—José de San Martín. Born in 1788 at Yapeyú in Argentina, San Martín served the Spanish King in Europe during the Napoleonic Wars. Returning to his homeland

in 1812, he became convinced that Argentine independence must be preserved, and that the way to do it was to drive Spain from South America. He therefore set about organizing and training an army whose purpose was to conquer Peru, the stronghold of Spanish power in America.

In 1817, San Martín led his troops in an heroic crossing of the Andes and stormed into Chile, where, with the aid of the Chilean patriot, Bernardo O'Higgins, he defeated the Spaniards in the Battle of Chacabuco. After another decisive victory in Chile, this time at Maipú, he boarded the ships of the Earl of Dundonald, a British naval officer in the service of the Chilean revolutionaries, and set sail with his men for Peru. Lima fell to him in 1821 and he was declared "Protector of Peru." The actual conquest of the rest of the Spanish possessions he left to Simón Bolívar, who freed the remainder of Peru and what is now Ecuador, Colombia, Bolivia, and Venezuela.

Juan Manuel de Rosas, although officially Governor of the Province of Buenos Aires, was actually dictator of the whole Argentine Confederation. He tried to conquer Uruguay but was overthrown when Brazil intervened and fled to England where he died in exile in 1877.

CIVIL STRIFE

While San Martín was leading his forces to victory, the territories of La Plata were torn by internal dissension, as the junta leaders broke into factions and fought one another. Santiago de Liniers and Alzaga were killed. Buenos Aires became the headquarters of the Unitarist Party, which sought to centralize control in the capital city and regulate the affairs of the outlying regions from there. In the cities of the interior the Federalist Party was dominant. Composed of ranchers for the most part, it aimed to limit the control of the merchants of Buenos Aires, and establish a federal union of the various regions of the country. Uruguay was occupied by the Brazilians while still struggling to sever its connection with Buenos Aires. Argentine trade and economic life came to a halt, and the country seemed destined to break up.

JUAN MANUEL DE ROSAS

In 1826, the Unitarist Party seemed victorious. Its members drew up a constitution which affirmed the control of Buenos Aires over the interior, and elected Bernardino Rivadavia president. With English and Argentine help, Uruguay was freed from the Brazilians and became independent at last. Then Rivadavia and the Unitarists were overthrown and the Federalists assumed control of the government. Their leader, Manuel Dorrego, was in turn assassinated in a Unitarist coup.

At this point, Juan Manuel de Rosas, a Federalist sympathizer, intervened, determined to put an end to civil war and unite his countrymen. Ruling as a dictator from 1829 until 1852, he often employed ruthless methods to quell dissent, and succeeded in concentrating political power in Buenos Aires, in spite of his Federalist

Ships of the Argentine Navy are depicted in a mid-19th-century painting.

A landmark of the capital is the statue of Christopher Columbus that stands near the Casa Rosada.

beginnings. He interfered in the affairs of Uruguay and Bolivia and antagonized England and France, causing the European nations to blockade Buenos Aires. Argentine trade suffered greatly as a result, and finally popular disapproval led to a rebellion headed by Justo José de Urquiza. With Brazilian aid, Urquiza forced Rosas into exile in 1852.

LATER 19TH CENTURY

In 1853, a convention met at Santa Fé and wrote a new constitution, patterned on that of the United States of America, under which a federal government was established and the central control of Buenos Aires was severely limited. Once again the issue of domination by the capital became a live one. The rich merchants of Buenos Aires were unwilling to accept the loss of privilege and power and refused to join the new Federation, maintaining a semi-independent status until 1862 when the city was re-united with the rest of Argentina, under the terms of a third constitution. In the meantime, the seat of the federal government had been shifted to the city of Paraná. It was now returned to Buenos Aires.

After half a century of disorder and dictatorship, Argentina now began to prosper. During the presidency of Bartolomé Mitre (1862–68), a great influx of German and Italian immigrants began. The new settlers opened up much of the pampa to agriculture, and wheat soon became a major crop.

During this period, Argentina set about consolidating its own territory. The remaining Indian tribes were beaten and scattered; railways were built; and the boundary with Chile was adjusted by treaty. The only foreign conflict of the times took place from 1865 to 1870, when Argentina joined Brazil and

Uruguay in the War of the Triple Alliance against Paraguay, an effort that resulted in the overthrow of the Paraguayan dictator, Francisco Solano López.

The remainder of the 19th century saw an unprecedented development of the nation's resources. The strain of Indian blood in the descendants of the early settlers was overwhelmed by new immigrants from Spain, the rest of Europe and the British Isles. Foreign trade flourished, irrigation schemes were realized in the arid west and the development of the country's vast agricultural wealth began.

THE 20TH CENTURY

Argentina entered the 20th century on a different footing from the rest of South America. The Indians within its borders had not lived in settled communities with large populations, as was the case in Peru and other countries. They were few in number and were almost entirely replaced by European immigrants. Thus Argentina did not follow the Latin American pattern of a huge Indian and *mestizo* (mixed) lower class ruled by a small white aristocracy. The temperate climate and abundance of rich soil attracted Old World farmers in huge numbers. In one important respect, however, the Argentine Republic resembled the other lands of South America—its economic basis was chiefly agricultural, not industrial.

THE TWO WORLD WARS

At first Argentina was hard-hit economically by World War I. Its huge export trade of meat, hides and grain was temporarily cut off, as was the flow into the country of badly needed manufactured goods, which its own industry could not provide. The Argentine Government declared its neutrality in 1914, then set about seeking manufactured goods from sources in the United States of America. Agricultural output was increased in order to help feed those European countries with whom wartime trade was maintained, and eventually to provide foodstuffs for all of Europe after the war. By the war's end, Argentina was still neutral and increasingly prosperous. This prosperity continued into the period between the two wars. In the 1920's, an economic boom was in progress, during which social legislation was enacted and public works projects launched on a wide scale.

The National Savings Bank is one of several huge banking institutions that make Buenos Aires the financial as well as the political capital.

By the 1930's a period of economic slump and social unrest had begun in Argentina as in much of the rest of the world. A trend towards conservative politics took place and dominated Argentine life through the outbreak of World War II. When hostilities broke out in Europe in 1939, Argentina once more declared itself neutral, and maintained diplomatic relations with the Axis Powers, Germany and Italy, although most other American countries severed ties with them.

JUAN DOMINGO PERON

Feelings within Argentina grew hot, as those who advocated strict neutrality confronted those who wished the Government to align itself with England, the United States, and the Allies. In addition, the large number of Argentines of Italian and German background included some whose sympathies were with the Axis. Then in 1943 a military junta seized control of the Government. A second military coup followed in 1944, bringing to the front a man who for many years was to lead Argentina—Juan Domingo Perón. Perón, an army officer, held a number of posts in the junta government, his influence steadily increasing. While his sympathies appeared to be with the Axis, Argentine national interest won out, for in 1945 the junta which he dominated at last declared war on Germany and Japan.

In 1946, Perón, who by now had enlisted strong popular support through promises of social and economic reform, was elected President of Argentina. Through the Labour Party which he organized, he came to dominate the trade unions. Later, through the National Revolutionary Party, he and his wife, Eva, succeeded in exerting a profound influence over Argentine life. Eva Perón especially was the object of mass demonstrations of support and affection by the workers of the large cities.

Perón's main contribution was his effort to develop Argentine industry and create a more balanced economy, no longer based mainly on agriculture. But, in seeking to achieve this end, he created new problems. The national debt mounted and the finances of the country became shakier. His restrictions on farm production caused serious resentment. He also made

Dr. Arturo Illía, President of Argentina (1963–66) attempted to restore democratic government to the country, but the freedom he permitted Peronistas and Communists alarmed many influential conservatives and moderates and led to his overthrow.

enemies of the Catholic Church and of many influential elements of Argentine society. Finally he was overthrown in 1955 (his wife had died in 1952), and took refuge in Spain.

THE PRESENT

After the fall of Perón, Argentina was ruled by a temporary military régime. The Peronista (National Revolutionary) Party was outlawed and, in 1958, Arturo Frondizi was elected to the presidency. His measures to cure the ills inherited from the Perón régime led to his own overthrow in 1962. A provisional President, José María Guido, replaced him until the election of Arturo Illía in 1963.

In the meantime, the Peronista forces were once more asserting themselves. In 1966, Illía was ousted and succeeded by a military junta headed by Lieutenant-General Juan Carlos Ongania. The junta claimed that Illía was not firm enough in checking the resurgence of the Peronistas.

A magnificent specimen marches by the crowd in the stand. Argentine "estancieros" (owners of large ranches) pay premium prices for bulls like this one, and the bidding at cattle auctions is lively.

The political instability of Argentina in recent years derives partly from the destruction of the traditional two-party system by Juan Perón, causing a splintering of the political and economic factions of the country—60 political parties were represented in the 1963 elections. At the same time, the still powerful Peronista movement has been kept from active participation in government for most of the period since Perón's downfall. This situation has sharply limited the ability of the Government to enlist popular backing in its efforts to cope with such serious problems as monetary inflation, foreign debts, and the need for industrial expansion.

In the shady dooryard of their simple farmhouse near Salta a farmer and his family entertain a visitor. These are true "criollos."

3. THE PEOPLE

THE 23,000,000 PEOPLE of Argentina are estimated to be 97 per cent of Caucasian stock, mainly Spanish and Italian. A very large number of them, however, are of other Old World origin—French, German, English, Scottish, Welsh, Basque, Irish, Polish, Lebanese, Greek, Dutch, Russian, Swiss and Hungarian.

Before the great waves of European settlers arrived in the 19th century, most of the population lived in the east central region near Buenos Aires. This part of the country is still the most densely populated, for it not only contains a number of the largest cities, but its surface is thick with small villages. However, irrigation opened up many parts of the interior to farming and many of the new immigrants have settled there. Sheep-raising and, later, petroleum exploitation, have brought many people into the chilly south, but population is still sparse in Patagonia and Tierra del Fuego.

Many picturesque groups typical of old Argentina have all but disappeared. Very little

Yahgan women and girls are busy making rope from grass.

In crude initiation lodges such as this, the Yahgans are introduced into full membership in the tribe.

trace remains of a once fairly numerous Negro population, brought in as slaves in colonial days; Indian tribes survive in Patagonia and other marginal areas, and Indian blood shows in the features of some of the people of the Gran Chaco and elsewhere in the extreme north; and the gauchos have largely disappeared as a distinct breed of men with their own rough-riding way of life and unique costume.

THE INDIANS

Apart from the Onas and Tehuelches of Patagonia, surviving Indians include the Yahgans and Alacalufs of Tierra del Fuego. All four of these tribes were among the most backward in the world at the time of the first European arrivals, and remained so into modern times. Half-naked, they fished and hunted in Argentina's bleak southern regions, occasionally wrapping capes of animal skins around themselves to keep out the chill wind.

The Tehuelches and the Onas were mainly hunters who stalked the guanaco on the Patagonian plateau. The Alacalufs and the Yahgans caught seals on the rocky coasts of Tierra del

A Yahgan Indian woman of Tierra del Fuego is hard at work making a bucket from bark. She is well covered with clothes, unlike her ancestors, who braved the chilly climate of Cape Horn with little or no clothing.

33

The blindfolded horse bucks but the gaucho coolly clings to his back. The men at the right wear peaked caps with their ballooning "bombachas" (trousers), a compromise between old and new.

Fuego. Handfuls of these people survive, although their ways have been modified by the introduction into their lands of sheep-raising by the white settlers—and many of them are now shepherds.

On the northern plains the tribes were more advanced and more warlike: they functioned rather in the manner of the North American Plains Indians. Learning white man's ways and adopting some of his tools, they presented a formidable threat to the settlers until they were finally overcome. In general, the pre-European population of Argentina was primitive, poorly organized and small in number—not at all like the Indians of Peru. Hunters rather than agriculturalists, they resisted assimilation and were quite indisposed to become native peasants under Spanish rule. Their descendants today, including part-Indians, number about 600,000. Pure-blooded Indians form only a small part of this total.

THE GAUCHOS

The modernization of Argentina's interior has made the traditional life of the gaucho virtually a thing of the past. The old gaucho was a frontiersman, living in a hostile environment and suspicious of the life of the cities. Like the cowboy of the North American West, he fought Indians and the forces of nature; he was self-reliant, extremely tough and distrustful of authority (although ready to follow a strong leader such as Rosas). His needs were extremely simple: often his boots were made of the hide of a colt just killed, the fresh skin being removed from the animal's hind leg and slipped over the gaucho's own leg and foot, there to dry and assume the shape of a boot. The gaucho's foot thus served as a last for making his own shoe!

The gaucho was a meat eater almost exclusively, living on beef fresh or jerked (*charqui*). He sipped Paraguay tea from a gourd, wore

The traditional gaucho boot made from pony hide ("bota de potro") usually had an aperture at the tip to allow freedom and mobility to the big toe. This style of footwear, which certainly emphasized the fact that the gaucho was a horseman rather than a pedestrian, may still be seen.

balloon trousers and a broad-brimmed hat and was uneasy when not on horseback. He scorned the new immigrants of the 19th century who swarmed into the pampa and fenced in the open range. The gaucho epitomized the native Argentine spirit of the colonial period, hostile to Spanish rule and conscious of Argentine nationality. The image of the gaucho has survived as an Argentine symbol—there is a whole literature glorifying him—although the gaucho breed is no longer either so numerous or so picturesque.

Today the gaucho is simply a *criollo*, or countryman. It is true that he still wears the *bombachas* (full breeches), but his boots are real ones, often ornamented with silver, and more likely than not he is just one employee among

The old-time gaucho scorned civilization and all its complications. For him, the simpler the equipment the better—he would have difficulty recognizing as fellow gauchos these modern men hosing down their mounts after the day's work.

Some "bombachas" are so long and full as to conceal the gaucho's feet entirely, as in the case of this man from Salta Province.

Like his North American counterpart, the gaucho runs down a steer.

Even farther removed from the true gaucho spirit of old is this man executing a gaucho dance in a Buenos Aires night club, the same sort of dance that his hard-bitten predecessors did round the campfire when the day's riding was done and night fell on the pampa.

With a steady hand and a sharp eye, an old "criollo" slices a thong from a piece of rawhide.

thousands of more ordinary ones engaged in the modern, scientific breeding and raising of Argentine beef.

THE CRIOLLOS

Much of the character of Argentine life, especially in the provinces of the interior derives from the *criollos* (Creoles). This term in colonial days meant a native of white or *mestizo* (mixed) blood. Later it was used to distinguish the Argentines of colonial descent from the offspring of the great 19th-century immigrations from Europe. However, the newcomers were readily absorbed, faster, perhaps, than in any other New World country, and *criollo* now means an Argentine through and through, usually a countryman or villager. The *criollo*, used to neglect by Spain and mismanagement

pean immigrants, dissatisfied with conditions in their home countries, found in Argentina a sense of nationality with which they could identify themselves, an American rather than a transplanted European tradition on which to build a new life.

THE ARTS

There is a pronounced French influence in Argentine cultural life. Although echoes of Spain are everywhere, Buenos Aires really resembles Paris more than Madrid, in the style of architecture, the tempo of city life, and the pursuit of cultural activities. Argentine painting and music owe as much to Paris, Vienna, and Berlin as to Spain. In the 19th century, Argentine intellectuals flocked to the great universities of northern and central Europe and returned to their native land to apply the concepts and techniques which they learned there.

Among many Argentines prominent in the arts are the sculptor Rogelio Yrurtia (1879–1950), known for the tomb of Commodore

by Spanish colonial administrators, developed a strong sense of self-reliance and in time a sense of being an Argentine, not a transplanted Spaniard. A spirit of the frontier is very much present in the Argentine national outlook. The Argentine is proud, hospitable, and courteous in the Spanish tradition, but there is an added element of frontier independence. The Euro-

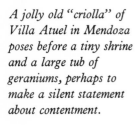

A jolly old "criolla" of Villa Atuel in Mendoza poses before a tiny shrine and a large tub of geraniums, perhaps to make a silent statement about contentment.

"Un Alto en el Camino" (A Stop on the Way) is one of the works of the 19th-century genre painter and portraitist, Prilidiano Pueyrredón.

Rivadavia; the brothers Beruti—Pablo (1870–1916), who wrote the opera *Cochabamba*, and Arturo (1862–1938), remembered for the opera *Pampa*; and the painter Prilidiano Pueyrredón (1823–70), a superior portraitist. The most famous composer is Alberto Williams (1862–1952), a student of César Franck, and founder of the Buenos Aires conservatory. An outstanding modern composer is Alberto Ginastera (1916–) whose opera *Bomarzo* has stunned audiences by its violent, spectacular quality.

Buenos Aires is a lively cultural capital, with

On a tree-lined boulevard in Buenos Aires, a flower-seller displays his wares to a pair of affluent carriage riders.

The National Museum of Art in Buenos Aires is one of the many cultural, educational and scientific institutions that make the city the rival of Madrid as hub of the Spanish-speaking world.

a year-round calendar of opera, ballet, concerts, and theatrical productions, many splendid museums, and a strong public interest in the arts.

Argentina is known as the home of the tango, a spirited dance in 4/4 time, which gained world-wide popularity in the years before World War I. Some authorities say the tango is of Spanish gypsy origin and was brought to Argentina by the Spanish settlers, where it took on a special quality. Others hold that it is derived from the *milonga*, a folk air of the Buenos Aires slums, influenced by Negro slave rhythms. There is no support for the belief that the tango resulted from the efforts of gauchos to waltz.

The horse plays a prominent rôle in Argentine life. Here a sculptor models a mare and foal in clay during the National Livestock Show in Buenos Aires.

The Gothic spires of the great pilgrimage shrine of Luján soar above the pampa near Buenos Aires.

RELIGION AND EDUCATION

Most Argentines are Roman Catholics, and while freedom of religion is guaranteed by the Constitution, the Catholic Church receives support from the Government. Protestants are relatively few in number, but the Jewish community, numbering nearly half a million, is by far the largest in Latin America, and second largest, after the United States of America, in the New World.

Education is free and compulsory between the ages of 6 and 14, and the illiteracy rate (less than 7 per cent of the population) is the lowest in Latin America. Compulsory public education is the responsibility of provincial govern-

The Colón Theatre, the Opera House of Buenos Aires, is the most imposing of the city's many theatres. In the number of productions staged annually Buenos Aires rivals New York and London.

In Buenos Aires, booksellers set up their portable stands and wait for strollers to come and browse, in a scene that recalls Paris.

ment, except in federal territory, such as Buenos Aires. Federal funds, however, help support the provincial school systems.

Secondary education is not required by law; however, most high schools (*colegios*, or for girls, *liceos*) are operated by the federal government, although some are under provincial control. Some *colegios* are attached to Argentine universities. All universities are public and receive federal support. The University of Córdoba, founded in 1613, is one of the oldest in the New World, and is older than many European universities (the University of Strasbourg, for example, dates from 1621).

LANGUAGE AND LITERATURE

Spanish is the official language of Argentina. However, Argentine Spanish has many points of difference with Castilian Spanish, especially in pronunciation. Second-generation speakers of European immigrant languages and those still using native Indian tongues are negligible in number. An interesting exception to this is the Welsh shepherd colony in Patagonia, who have largely resisted assimilation, and still preserve the Welsh language. Buenos Aires is

In the courtyard of the Colegio Nacional in Buenos Aires, students stroll between classes. Secondary schools such as this are very similar to the "lycées" of France in organization and curriculum.

In a classroom of a simple country school in the north, where most of Argentina's surviving Indians and mestizos live, a "European" and an Indian boy share a desk.

one of the world's main points of dissemination of information in the Spanish language, and for many years surpassed Madrid and Barcelona in the volume of books published. Printing and publishing are still major activities in Argentina.

Argentina has fathered a large number of writers, many of whom are widely read in other Spanish-speaking countries. Of earlier writers, among the best known are Gregorio Funes (1749–1830), author of a standard work on Argentine history, *Ensayo de la Historia Civil del Paraguay, Buenos Aires y Tucumán*; José Marmol (1818–70), who wrote the novel *Amalia* about the dictatorship of Rosas (who banished him); and Bartolomé Mitre, known

Dr. José C. Paz founded the world-famous Buenos Aires newspaper, "La Prensa," in 1896. Reputed for its high standards of journalism, "La Prensa" was taken over by the Perón régime, which it opposed, but was restored to its owners in 1955.

43

This massive structure is the Faculty of Law and Social Sciences at the University of Buenos Aires. Argentina has produced several distinguished jurists of international reputation.

not only as President of Argentina, but remembered for historical works such as his *Historia de San Martín*.

Other writers are José Hernandez (1834–86), who vividly depicted gaucho life in his famous novel, *Martín Fierro*; Ricardo Guiraldes (1886–1927), whose *Don Segundo Sombra* ranks among the greatest of gaucho novels; and Jorge Luis Borges (1899–), acclaimed by some as the greatest living writer in Spanish for his enigmatic, haunting works such as *Labyrinths* and *Ficciones*.

In the 1960's Julio Cortázar (1914–) gained international acclaim for his novels, "Hopscotch," "The Winners," and "The End of the Game."

MEN OF ACHIEVEMENT

Argentina has produced many outstanding leaders in the sciences and humanities. The distinguished jurist, Carlos Saavedra Lamas (1880–1959), won the Nobel Peace Prize in 1936 for his rôle in ending the Chaco War between Bolivia and Paraguay.

Another renowned jurist, Luis María Drago (1859–1921) who served on the Hague Tribunal, was a strong advocate of the Drago Doctrine. This doctrine was formulated by another Argentine jurist, Carlos Calvo (1824–1906) and therefore more properly called the Calvo Doctrine. It repudiated armed intervention by

This modern building, part of the Faculty of Sciences, is at the University of Buenos Aires. Argentine astronomers, mathematicians and physicists have made significant contributions to world scientific knowledge.

Boating is a popular pastime in the environs of Buenos Aires.

European powers in American nations in debt to them.

In 1947 another Nobel Prize went to Bernardo Houssay (1887–) for his research in medicine while director of the world-famous Institute of Biology and Experimental Medicine in Buenos Aires.

The great zoologist, German Burmeister (1807–92), was born in Germany. Coming to Argentina, he founded the Museum of Natural History in Buenos Aires, where he carried out important studies on fossils. Also known for his research in the same field is Italian-born Fiorino Ameghino (1854–1911).

A host of other Argentines have contributed to the knowledge of modern mankind. Of the many scientific institutions in Argentina, the observatories of Córdoba and La Plata are internationally known for their researches on the skies of the southern hemisphere. The Institutes of Mathematics at Buenos Aires and Rosario have been world leaders in such mathematical fields as topology, the theory of functions and mathematical physics.

SPORTS

Argentines are very sports-minded. While soccer is the national sport, horse-racing is a close second. Argentine racetracks are among the world's best and a large segment of the public lives, breathes, and talks horses. Sports involving horsemanship, such as polo and the rough-and-tumble sport called *pató*, are extremely popular.

Clubs and sporting associations thrive everywhere, and golf, tennis, swimming and other water sports have large followings. Argentina has produced champions in all activities. The splendid natural facilities of the rural areas offer limitless opportunities for hiking, camping, hunting and fishing. The long coastline and many lakes are ideal for yachting and boating. The delightful climate of much of the country encourages life out-of-doors.

A "pató" player swoops down and retrieves the ball.

Horse shows are a prominent feature of Argentine life. For many years Argentine teams have shown to advantage in international competitions.

The horse-loving Argentines are fond of "pató," an energetic and risky sport that is rather like mounted basketball. Note that the ball is equipped with handles on all sides.

Soccer or "futbol" is the national sport of Argentina, as it is in so many other countries. Here, in Buenos Aires, a great crowd watches a moment of exciting action.

Horse and rider gracefully clear the hurdle.

In Chubut Province, the fishing is first rate, as evidenced by the size of the trout this gamekeeper is holding.

Yerba mate, or Paraguay tea, is a native American stimulating drink that has been widely adopted by the Argentines. Here a city workman takes it in the traditional fashion, sipped through a tube from a gourd or gourd-shaped vessel.

FOOD

The Argentines are a well-nourished people. The natural bounty of their land assures that. Beef is the basis of the Argentine diet—many people eat it three times a day.

In Jujuy Province, "mestizo" workers in the sugar-cane fields take time out for lunch.

The apple harvest in Río Negro Province is an important event, for this region produces some of the world's finest apples.

Open-air barbecues are frequent, often featuring *asado con cuero*, an entire steer roasted underground with the hide left on, or on a more modest scale, *asado al asador*, an entire lamb barbecued. A meal may begin with *empanadas*, little pastries filled with meat, fish or other seafood, or these dainties may be served as snacks. *Puchero*, a stew of chicken, chickpeas, marrow bones and vegetables, is a more homely dish. Other substantial preparations are *carbonada criolla*, a hearty soup of meat and potatoes, or rice, and onions; and *locro*, a casserole of sausage, vegetables and maize.

Coffee, yerba mate, beer and the good domestic wines of Río Negro and Mendoza are the customary beverages.

The Presidential Palace or Casa Rosada (Pink House) is the official residence of the President of the Argentine Republic.

4. GOVERNMENT

ALTHOUGH, IN 1966, President Ongania dissolved the Argentine Parliament and Supreme Court, suspended political parties, and initiated rule by decree, Argentina is still technically a federal republic governed by the Constitution of 1853, as amended in 1860 and 1956. The 1956 change simply annulled a 1949 amendment whereby greater powers were given to the President (Juan Perón) at the expense of the other branches of the government.

The Argentine government was organized by the framers of the Constitution as a federal system whose highest powers reside in an Executive, a Legislative, and a Judicial Branch. This is the system of checks and balances on which the United States Constitution is based.

Its purpose is to prevent any individual from assuming too much power.

Since it is the stated objective of President Ongania in instituting rule by decree, to restore his country's economic well-being, it is to be assumed that a return to constitutional government will eventually take place.

EXECUTIVE

As provided by the Constitution of 1853–60, the President is elected for a term of 6 years, may not serve two successive terms, and must be a Roman Catholic. The President is assisted by the Vice President and a cabinet of 8 or more Ministers, and both President and his cabinet are subject to checks by the legislature.

The Argentine Congress is housed in the Capitol, a neo-classical structure whose huge cupola extends 279 feet above the ground.

LEGISLATURE

The Legislature consists of two houses, an upper and a lower. The upper house or Senate is composed of two delegates from each province and two from the Federal District of Buenos Aires. Senators are chosen by the members of the provincial legislatures. Members of the lower house, or Chamber of Deputies, are elected directly by the people, and their number is not fixed, since representation in the Chamber is based on the national census. Roughly, there is one deputy for 100,000 people. Under normal or constitutional procedure (in abeyance since 1966, it must be remembered), the Legislature is empowered to impeach the President, Vice President and cabinet members. The President may veto laws passed by the Legislature, but by a two-thirds vote in each house the veto may be over-ridden. All of these procedures are very similar to those of the government of the United States of America.

THE PROVINCES

The Provinces of Argentina correspond to the States of the United States of America. Each Province has its self-elected governor and legislature and assumes responsibility for all matters not delegated by the Constitution to the Federal Government.

Argentina has had several official names, some reflecting the federal structure of the government—the Argentine Republic, the United Provinces of the Río de la Plata, and the Argentine Confederation. The federal structure, however, has often been weakened by abuse of the power of the President to intervene in provincial government—dissolve legislatures, remove governors from office—when, in the opinion of himself and the federal Legislature, the national interest demands it.

The Provinces of Argentina are: Buenos Aires, Catamarca, Chaco, Chubut, Córdoba, Corrientes, Entre Ríos, Formosa, Jujuy, La

Pampa, La Rioja, Mendoza, Misiones, Nequén, Santa Cruz, Río Negro, Salta, San Juan, San Luis, Santa Fé, Santiago del Estero, and Tucumán. Tierra del Fuego constitutes a Federal Territory.

FOREIGN POLICY

Argentina is represented in many international organizations, a natural 'effect of the country's world-wide trade. A member of both the United Nations and the Organization of American States, Argentina is also a participant in the Alliance for Progress, the plan for technical assistance and mutual aid launched by President John F. Kennedy in 1961 at the Punta del Este Conference. Argentina was a founding member of the Latin American Free Trade Area, a preliminary step taken in 1961 towards creating a Latin American Common Market similar to that of West Europe.

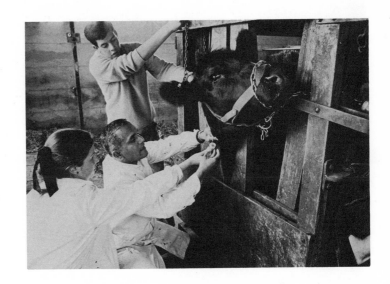

The quality of Argentina's cattle is constantly being improved. Here, under United Nations auspices, an animal health specialist from India takes blood samples from an ailing cow.

The vast meat-processing plants of Argentina send beef and other meat products to the entire world. Here a checker inspects the grading marks on beef carcasses.

5. THE ECONOMY

INDUSTRY

Until World War I, Argentine manufacturing was limited mainly to the processing of food and other items such as leather, produced on the land. With imports of manufactured goods from Europe cut off by the war, Argentina started to produce some other manufactured goods of its own. World War II brought about an even greater expansion in Argentine industry. However, the bulk of factory output is still sugar, flour and cereal products, wine, meat, leather goods, cotton, vegetable oils, and dairy products—all agricultural in origin.

Other industries that have developed are rubber, glass, ceramics, drugs, cement and assembly of foreign-made motor vehicles.

Heavy industry has long been limited by the country's dependence on foreign sources of fuel. Although domestic petroleum output has grown considerably, and the use of natural gas as well, these and the greatly expanded hydro-electric power system are not yet sufficient to foster the full development of heavy industry needed to offset the dominance of farming in the nation's economy. Buenos Aires and its immediate area contain the greater part of Argentine industry.

TRADE AND FINANCE

Argentina is one of the world's great trading nations, but the country's trade is lop-sided—90 per cent of its exports consists of agricultural produce—mainly beef, lamb, mutton,

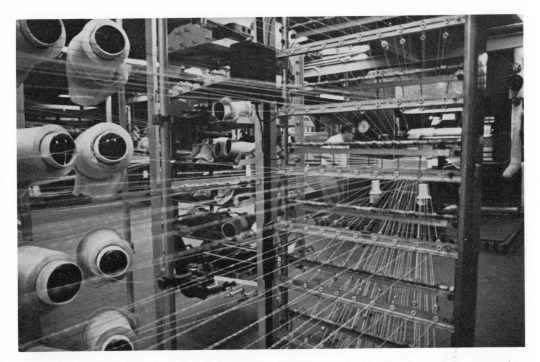

The raw material of rayon, cellulose, leaves a shredder in the Ducilo plant at Berazategui.

wheat, leather, and linseed oil—while most of its needs in machinery and equipment, iron and steel, chemicals and fuel must be imported.

Before World War II, the balance of trade was to Argentina's advantage, that is, the country took in more money from its exports than it paid out for imports. Since then the balance has fluctuated, the advantage being lost, except for some years, as in 1963 and 1964, when it was temporarily regained.

A gleaming Argentine freighter with passenger accommodation docks at the port of Buenos Aires.

Workmen prepare to install wheels on a tractor coming off the assembly line in the Fiat Concord plant at Córdoba.

A slashing machine finishes rayon yarn and winds it on to large bobbins ready for shipment to the weaving mills.

Women workers in the Fiat Matafer plant at Córdoba make seat covers and upholstery for new diesel railway cars being manufactured by Fiat at other plants in the same area.

Meat is transferred from the plant to waiting trucks.

Argentina has a large foreign debt incurred from borrowing money abroad to finance public works and industrial expansion, and to meet the balance-of-trade gap. The country's finances have suffered also from inflation—prices and costs mounting, and the value of the peso, the Argentine currency unit, decreasing.

England and Italy are the biggest consumers of Argentine goods, the former country being traditionally the chief market for the prize beef of the pampa. The United States, the Low Countries, Brazil and West Germany are other leading customers of Argentina.

TRADE UNIONS

The trade union movement in Argentina is well organized, with 2,500,000 of the nation's 6,000,000 workers belonging to the Central Labour Confederation, but influenced by the Peronistas, who control one of the two major wings of the Confederation. Communists have been a minor, but noisy faction. Before the Ongania régime the Communist party was legal, but had fewer than 100,000 members, although its sympathizers were estimated to exceed that number. President Ongania, upon assuming power, took immediate measures to curb the power of the trade unions, outlawing some of them, and freezing their funds. The outlawed unions were in six key industries—metallurgy, sugar, textiles, chemicals, transport, and communications. General strikes were formally banned. The unions retaliated by calling for an

The trucks roll up to the docks where the meat is put aboard a ship bound for Europe. On the wharf, an official checks the export authorization of a meat shipment.

57

The National Steel Works at San Nicolas on the Paraná River was inaugurated in 1960 in a bid to develop Argentina's heavy industry. This workman is employed in extracting slag from one of the mill's blast furnaces.

Hides have been one of the chief exports passing through the docks of Buenos Aires since colonial days. Here, a bundle of skins is lifted aboard a freighter.

Existing power plants have been enlarged. Workers are seen building an extension to the Puerto Nuevo plant designed to increase power output by one-half.

The chimneys of a sugar mill in Jujuy belch smoke as the raw cane is processed. Sugar production, located in the northern provinces, is a major Argentine industry.

Choice Argentine fruit is loaded aboard a ship on its way to European markets.

Skilled technicians staff the master control room of the Puerto Nuevo thermal power plant. In recent years, construction of thermal power plants has greatly increased Argentina's electrical output.

Overhauling the nation's transport system is a priority item on the Argentine agenda. At Córdoba a traffic control specialist directs all traffic in the city's railway station and marshalling yards.

Prize Hereford bulls are paraded before the judges at the National Livestock Show in Buenos Aires. This event is one of the major dates on the calendar in Argentina.

anti-government action campaign, but the union attitude was in fact rather one of watchful waiting until Ongania's policies for economic reform developed to the point of success or failure.

AGRICULTURE

The pampa ranks with Iowa and the Ukraine as one of the greatest reservoirs of fertile topsoil on the face of the earth. It is so rich that most pampa farmers find it unnecessary to use fertilizer.

The first Spanish settlers introduced cattle and horses. These animals throve on the splendid grass of the plains and multiplied rapidly with little care. It was not until much later that the full value of the pampa soil was realized, and much of the open cattle range was fenced and turned over to wheat and maize. Until then, Argentina, possessing some of the world's best land for growing wheat, imported the grain needed to make bread. The bursting fields of the pampa, which now produce enough wheat to feed all of Argentina and much of

Scientific cattle-raising, as exemplified by this calf being weighed, has greatly altered the life of the gaucho.

Yerba mate is infused from the leaves of a native species of holly. The leaves are stripped from the low shrubby tree and gathered into bales.

The bales of yerba mate are weighed before being sent out.

The faces of the spectators reflect their keen interest in the cattle being exhibited at the National Livestock Show. Improvement of breeding stock is serious business in Argentina.

A little boy in Jujuy Province grasps a stalk of cane. It is in the hollow stalk that the sweet juice is found from which the granulated sugar of the household is refined.

the rest of the world, rank seventh in world output. Argentina is also a world leader in maize (corn). Other cereals grown are oats, barley, and rye.

LIVESTOCK

The temperate climate, excellent pasturage and good water supply of the ranch country are ideally suited to the raising of fine cattle—an estimated 40,000,000 in 1967. Argentine cattlemen are among the world's most scientific breeders of prime beef, notably Black Angus and Hereford. Modern breeding began in the late 19th century when England became the chief buyer of pampa beef. The finest pedigreed stock available was imported to improve the domestic herds, and ever since then stockmen have not ceased their efforts to maintain the superior quality of Argentine beef. The same care is employed in raising sheep and pigs, both important to the Argentine economy. Argentine horses, famous on the polo fields and racetracks of the world, are bred on scientifically-run stud farms on the pampa.

The Provinces of Buenos Aires, La Pampa, Córdoba, Entre Ríos, and Santa Fé are the main livestock producers.

FRUIT

The Argentine climate is well suited to the raising of both temperate and sub-tropical fruits, and orchard crops are a major industry. Some of the best apples, plums, and pears grow in the cooler regions of Nequén, Río Negro, Mendoza, and San Juan. Buenos Aires Province, Entre Ríos, Corrientes and Santa Fé specialize in peaches, quinces and plums.

Sugar cane is a giant grass, like maize and bamboo. A worker in the field is dwarfed by the tall plants.

Gauchos pause before a field of sunflowers, whose huge nodding heads contain seed from which a commercially important oil is extracted.

A worker in the cane fields carries freshly cut cane on his shoulder.

Mendoza is famous for its olive groves, the "Mesopotamian" provinces for citrus fruits, and Salta for cherimoyas (custard apples). The grape thrives in the irrigated vineyards of sunny Mendoza, as well as farther south in Río Negro. Wine is important in these areas, and much of it is of very good quality. It does not, however, figure as an item of export—almost all of the output of the vineyards is consumed by the Argentines themselves.

OTHER CROPS

A crop of great economic importance in the pampa provinces is flax, grown not for the textile industry but for its seed, from which linseed oil is pressed. Only the United States of America and Russia surpass Argentina in flax-seed production. Cotton and sugar cane are the chief crops of the warmer northern provinces.

63

Thanks to the Gran Chaco, where almost all its cotton is grown, Argentina ranks among the world's largest producers of this basic crop.

The sword-like leaves of sugar cane are often seen not only in the Gran Chaco, but in other warm-climate provinces—Salta, Jujuy, and Tucumán where sugar is a major product.

Peanuts, tobacco, sunflower seed, alfalfa, flowers and flowering bulbs are other important farm crops.

OUTLOOK

In order to cure the economic depression and financial instability that has plagued Argentina for so long, Ongania set several objectives. First, he announced that the unregulated attempt to expand industry at the expense of agriculture, dating from the time of Perón, was to be halted, and government aid was to be granted to farmers and cattlemen. Next, he devalued the peso from 215 to the U.S. dollar to a fluctuating value between 245 and 255 to a dollar. He then invited foreign investment, guaranteeing protection to foreign firms established in Argentina. Next, a plan for reorganizing Argentine transport went into effect, in order to step up the efficiency of port handling and modernize outmoded rail facilities.

The regrettable suspension of democratic procedures that was required to bring these measures into effect did not produce too great opposition. The reaction of Argentines seemed to be one of acceptance in the hope that the country's serious difficulties would be overcome by these drastic measures, and that their country would take its place among the world's more dynamic nations—a place which it certainly merits on the basis of human and material resources.

Descendants of the famous gypsies of Spain found their way to Argentina, like this girl at an encampment near Córdoba.